IMPRISONED IN
THE GLOBAL CLASSROOM

IMPRISONED IN THE GLOBAL CLASSROOM

Ivan Illich
and
Etienne Verne

Writers and Readers

London　　New York　　Toronto　　Sydney

Writers and Readers Publishing Cooperative Ltd.
144a Camden High Street, London NW1
175 Fifth Avenue, New York, NY 10010
Imprisoned in the Global Classroom is reproduced from the Times
Educational Supplement by permission.
Published by Writers and Readers Publishing Cooperative Ltd. 1976.
Reprinted 1981.

Printed in Canada by The Hunter Rose Co. Ltd., Toronto

SBN 0 904613 30 5
LC# 81-51546

Contents

IMPRISONED IN
THE GLOBAL CLASSROOM

Ivan Illich and Etienne Verne

An analysis of the defects of the school system no longer stirs anyone to action. This is true of the specialists who establish the facts, the politicians who decide how to dress them up, and the teachers who have to come to terms with them. The conclusions reached are deposited in libraries, and the great international bureaucracies have taken on the task of disseminating them.

The general agreement on the growing inefficiency of increasing educational expenditure, at an increasingly high social cost, is both dangerous and perverse. Dangerous, in that it justifies the formulation of new educational policies, and maintains the power of those agencies and networks whose function it is to adopt and implement them. Perverse, in that the more the various criticisms of the school system are absorbed, the more deeply rooted becomes the idea that education is necessary, mandatory and never-ending.

The greater the agreement on the futility of exorbitant educational expenditure, on the social poverty which it perpetuates and conceals, and on the frustration which it encourages, the greater the ingenuity used to find new resources and provide more money for alternative educational budgets. This is taken as far as a compulsory contribution from the French worker to provide for a training which he does not want, from which he hardly benefits, but which serves to adapt, integrate, tame and dominate him.

It is not usually drawn to our attention that this training is to be provided by 'instructors', a new profession, the development of which has the particular advantage of providing jobs for intellectuals who would otherwise be unemployed. It also ensures that an alliance between intellectuals and working men remains obstructed by the system. Permanent education absorbs the 40,000 intellectuals for whom no other job exists, and employs them as 'instructors', course designers, directors and inspectors of education.

Their deployment in permanent education as full-time 'instructors' ensures that they do not become a discontented group, drifting on the fringe of industrial institutions. By making them into a profession, by confirming their university status and by defending their rights, and later their monopoly, permanent education recruits them into the process of renewing the work force.

The workers will find themselves at an even greater disadvantage at the hands of a class of professional monopolists, of community therapists, and specialists in communication and management. Thus the 'instructors' will deal the same blow to the individual worker's autonomy as the professional politicians dealt to his fighting capacity.

When analysing the various dimensions of the worldwide crisis in education, when denouncing the mounting cost of educational programmes, and exposing the hidden curriculum, it was universally assumed that the main result of this destructive criticism of the 10 or 15 years' compulsory school attendance and of continuing full-time schooling would be the acceptance of the idea of permanent education, instruction for people of all ages, and the throwing open of educational institutions.

It was probably the examination of alternative solutions to the negative effects of schooling that led away from the concept of education restricted to the early years of life to that of continuing educational support.

Because they limit their attention to the evident consequences of compulsory schooling, rather than to the hidden curriculum and the social ethos it produces, politicians can never think further than compensating for, correcting or restricting its superficial failings.

But the one certain effect of these innovations is to conceal still further the latent programme merely by manipulating the manifest facts, and thereby reinforcing it. Research by experts into alternative strategies, and the imposition by politicians of new legislation and regulations, imply that individuals and communities have neither sufficient resources to discover their particular educational requirements, nor the power to decide for themselves how to meet their needs. At every turn they become a little more alienated from themselves and a little more industrialized. This, in fact, is the universal result of compulsory schooling.

The fact that the technocrats have been converted from the traditional school system to the idea of permanent education is the best illustration of this transfer from a limited to an unlimited endless education, and the best evidence of the extension of their power. Now that the technocrats have appropriated it for themselves, permanent education can never be a plan for breaking up formal schooling in a significant social context.

A few years ago the extension of education to every period of life was freely offered as a radical alternative to schooling and a means of limiting its growth. There appeared to be two complementary aims: the deschooling of educational processes and the introduction of permanent education.

These aims were complementary, in that one could scarcely expect permanent education to be launched on a major scale without the imposition of corresponding limits on the development of schooling, or even its reduction. Limits on school policies became necessary on these grounds :

Economic: limitation of educational expenditure and need for increased cost-effectiveness.

Social: the perpetuation of social inequality and the absence of a redistribution of opportunity.

Political: the increasing inability of school and universities to persuade students to adjust and be subjugated by the industrial mode of creating wealth.

Ethical: the increasingly powerful 'imperialism' of the school label, dominating the right of individuals and groups to decide for themselves how they want to live and manage their relationship to the production process.

Strategically, on the management level, the proclaimed permanence of access to education and the right to receive instruction was calculated to make it easier for the political bureaucracies to accept limitations on the quantitative development of schooling, since educational opportunity would not be restricted to the early years, everyone being offered a second or even a third chance. This is prime territory for the philosophy of equality of opportunity.

The fact is that the development of schooling was compromised when it became difficult to find means of increasing education budgets without further prejudice to other developing sectors, and when doubts about economic productivity and the social justifiability of this expenditure compelled attention.

11

At the time, educationists and politicians were presenting permanent education not as a new approach to teaching, but as a new social model which would seek official respectability either through the prestige of the cultural revolution; or in the mists of the permanent revolution; or within the utopian framework of a new society yet to be established; or, again, in the more voluntarist perspective of a political struggle which allows us to choose today what we want tomorrow.

The task is to prove that these projects (no matter how well they are defended) are an expression of the modern, humanistic, educational illusion, according to which the order of things and the characteristics of institutions will change if man's education is changed. When society is stratified, and the distribution of capital is the yardstick of its stratification, it is constantly necessary to encourage people to believe in the redistribution of opportunity, and therefore to endorse the essential character of its inequality, so that those who hold power can then justify their position.

Once a division has been made between social and technical aspects of work, it is necessary to ensure that the acquisition of qualifications is progressive, and that these qualifications are not only differentiated, but separate. For reasons relating to the current economic situation and to the state of development of industrial production, it has become important to transfer some functions which the school no longer performs adequately to permanent education.

Deschooling, which has been adopted by the ideology of industry, assists this transfer, just as various fascist regimes today are assisted by self-conscious rationalization. In the same way that deschooling is used to promote education without schools and schools without walls, education satellites and the knowledge industry, teaching machines and multi-media systems, it is used to promote permanent education. Without doubt, deschooling here falls into a most dangerous and well-concealed trap, laid for it by those who wish to utilize it to justify the educational megamachine of the year 2000.

If permanent education is simply the expression of an educational illusion, we will still need to prove that it must inevitably lead to a repeat of the same consequences as the original

12

expression of this illusion in an industrial society, namely schooling. As an embodiment of schooling, a permanent education policy will never be anything but a trap for any plan for deschooling society.

The lines of argument are various but clear. They start with the description of schooling as unavoidable, the detailed workings of permanent education and the perpetuation of the material foundations of the institution of schooling. And they range through to the persistent nursing, through schooling, of the idea of education as a compulsory instrument of mediation between the individual's desire to learn and what he desires to learn. Other arguments include the fact that permanent education reproduces the same consequences as school and reinforces its social functions.

With the spread of the industrialization of education, and the commercialization of knowledge, it amounts, basically, to bringing back the hidden curriculum of schooling and confirming its obvious consequences. Among these I particularly draw attention to one, which ensures that permanent education becomes not the symbol of our unfinished development, but a guarantee of our permanent inadequacy.

In mercantile societies the idea of education underwent a first transformation, as it came to mean the manipulation of one individual by another, or the unreciprocated influence of one individual over another. The alchemists gave a spatial picture of this process, and successfully programmed its successive phases.

Industrial societies transformed the idea of education a second time; by education they meant the manipulation of children by adults using a programmed instrument called the school. In permanent education we are no doubt witnessing a further reduction of the idea of education, this time for the exclusive benefit of the capitalists of knowledge and the professionals licensed to distribute it.

We need no longer ask ourselves if the general extension of education to all ages and the availability of teaching equipment at different stages of life are merely phenomena illustrating how all education is contaminated by school procedures. Now that the subjection of childhood to pedagogy via the school has been accomplished, it remains to complete the process by extending it

13

to adulthood.

In fact, and from a historical point of view, one gets the general impression that the aim is to extend the institution of childhood into adulthood. By subjecting adults to pedagogy, the perpetuation of childhood is instigated; a process of puerilization takes place. Few classes of healthy first-formers would fail to make merciless fun of anyone attempting to give them training exercises in sales techniques, which instructors of adults inflict on staff, who know that their security depends on their docility in admiringly conforming to the rules.

Adult schooling will be the instrument used for this process of transforming the social definition of adulthood. The aim of school could be said to be the acquisition of adulthood. Once the majority have been convinced that they have no claim to maturity, permanent education asserts itself as an unending process, and hence as an indispensable tool.

Medicine has followed the converse process of development : after medicalizing death, it succeeded in medicalizing life, and then birth. The school first dealt with access to adult and working life. Now it aims to accompany the worker throughout his working life, to the point of teaching retired people to agree not to work and to occupy their time. Medicine has made life the subject of medical care; education makes existence the subject of a study course.

Just as suffering has been medicalized, existence has been scholarized, and even becomes the subject of an apprenticeship. The medical profession, in forcing people to be born and die in hospital, succeeded in inculcating the idea that life is a disease. Now professional educators, through the institution of permanent education, succeed in convincing men of their permanent incompetence. The ultimate success of the schooling instrument is the extension of its monopoly, first to all youth, then to every age and, finally, to all areas.

Here, one would have to be in a position to designate the social, political and economic conditions for the 'discovery' of adulthood as an object of pedagogical attention, that is as a particular age occupying a definite position in and relating to the school curriculum. It would also be the object of specific

14

pedagogical action which will make the 'job of being a pupil' the only secure occupation throughout life, particularly at times when people have no other employment.

To talk of the 'permanent job of being a pupil' amounts to announcing the various prices which have to be paid to the industrial mythologies to secure the development of endless education.

We have reached that decisive moment in the history of education at which the great international agencies have already formulated their plans for subjecting the entire life of everyone to schooling, more often than not in the furtherance of 'making deschooling a necessity by any means available'. We have also reached the point when various countries, from underindustrialized Peru to overindustrialized France, are beginning to back permanent education with legislation.

The institutionalization of permanent education must reproduce and improve the dissemination of the procedures programmed in the initial stages of education, and provide for the inculcation of their hidden curriculum.

The *cholo* from Chimbote and the semi-skilled worker at the Renault works in Boulogne-Billancourt will be given the clear impression that they have at all times the possibility of climbing the social ladder, with the help of the training and the educational resources which have been assigned to them. They will have the permanent knowledge that the opportunity to reach the top of the ladder is always there, and that it is entirely due to their own deficiencies if they fail to grasp it.

The education pundits have a fine prospect before them, as they can allow themselves to retranscribe for adult education the same chapters about final aims, mechanisms and consequences as those already written for schooling; there is nothing so like an international conference on the education of children as an international conference on the education of adults. The chapters are the same: the education of adults as a factor in spreading democracy, the education of adults as a development factor, equality of access and equality of opportunity, the education of the most disadvantaged adults, and so on.

The only true form of deschooling is the one that cannot be programmed. Real deschooling is going on in schools and univer-

15

sities, as evidenced by dropping out, absenteeism, the increasing irrelevance of what takes place in them, and 'allergy to work'.

The schools and universities are producing the hoped-for results less and less often; they are less and less able to perform the social functions assigned to them; their deterioration is increasingly obvious and their irrelevance is becoming more serious; they are less 'efficient' and less competent to reproduce the conditions of industrial production.

It is becoming urgent that the same social forces which introduced compulsory schooling should transfer the functions that the initial stages of education provide increasingly badly, to the field of adult education. This will be done by restoring to the centre of the production process activities which are drifting away from it, or which had developed on its periphery, as with the popular education movements.

One of the most obvious consequences of the French Laws passed in July 1971 on 'continuous vocational training through permanent education' is to have again made the centre of the company the locale for educational activity, through the influence of the compulsory financing of training. In this way a return to the tradition of 'factory schools', which underwrote the prosperity of early days of capitalism, is effected. This is also the meaning of the reintroduction of apprenticeship in France since 1971.

The panel on youth which met early in 1974 in the United States under the auspices of the President's Science Advisory Committee also followed the same line when it recommended the more rapid integration of young people of school age into the working world. The impression is that the demands of industrial democracy on the educational tool are becoming increasingly pressing and increasingly hectic, to ensure the survival of the industrial age.

The institutionalization of permanent education, therefore, has the effect of gathering together and formalizing a whole set of informal activities, of tagging the educational label on to a whole set of spontaneous gestures and behaviour patterns. It even presents as a normal and morally healthy thing the creation of a 'continuing sex education training and research centre', where,

16

according to the publicity for this new product from the instructor, people can 'explore by experience the various aspects of emotional and sexual life in live situations'.

These are activities and behaviour patterns which have been going on for a long time, although they have hitherto escaped the legal recognition of the lawyers, the planning of the politicians, the investigation of the analyists, the programming of the educators, the medicalization of the doctors, and the appraisal of the social controllers.

In the old days, the planner merely had to talk with his colleagues round his drawing board to solve his problems. Today he cannot discuss them in his firm, but must leave his place of work to listen to a specialist in a specially equipped room, at a programmed time, who will tell him about subjects he has not come across and will teach him how to solve problems which he does not have.

It is not for nothing that the percentage of training courses organized directly by firms is rising, or that most training courses programmed for manual and supervisory workers are courses in 'the knowledge and discovery of the firm'. This is the kind of course which was programmed for the Lip workers in Grenoble when the strike ended.

When institutionalization appears, the personnel manager, the works council, the book-keeper and the instructor may well be aware of this stupidity; they can only extricate themselves by planning, financing and perpetuating it.

It is no different for the Callao fisherman who, caught in the net of an 'educational nucleus', has to accept educational resources that are decided for him. Thus, popular education movements, mesmerized by the financial resources offered them by the permanent education legislators, agree to submit to the rules of the financial inspectors, to the criteria of the legal administrators, and to the selections of the purveyors of knowledge.

So what action should be taken? The following list contains suggestions for identifying the crucial obstacles, as well as some of the solutions to be recommended and the abuses to the condemned :

1. Show up the disguising of the compulsory nature of adult education which lies behind the obligation on firms to finance education activities. This obligation reinforces all the definitions of competence, and qualifications based only on a recognition derived from reaching a given stage in a school curriculum, and the validation of this position by means of an examination.

2. Condemn the excessive influence of industry on this training, achieved by allowing firms to organize, administer and validate independently the training they give to their workers. Transferring state education budgets to industry is not a step forward. It still leaves individuals, workers and communities deprived of power over education.

3. Make it illegal to require a person applying for a job to produce school or university diplomas or training course certificates, or to take psychological tests.

4. Reject any right to training determined on the exclusive basis of the position held or to be held in the industrial system. Protest against the immorality of compulsorily spending a part of the workers' money for the purpose of bringing them to a state of subjection by linking promotion with training, and by making them think that by introducing formal training the industrial undertaking will become a vehicle of education.

5. Ban additional educational expenditure serving to maintain the status, power and prestige of people whose training has already cost the public most. Manual and supervisory workers must be in a position to follow the same courses and at equal cost. Having compelled workers to sell their labour, the aim of the industrial undertaking is to make them believe that 'human assets' can be treated in the same way as physical assets, and that education can be quantified in order to infer more convincingly that it is a marketable commodity.

6. Resist the professionalization of full-time instructors.

7. Banish educational tools not designed by the individuals concerned.

8. Reject any training policy which is presented as an employ-

ment policy, either with a view to restocking the workforce and adapting it to different jobs, or as a regulator of the labour market. More training is not the solution to the current employment difficulties. It is more important to eliminate the frustration that training induces in the workers, than to increase their productivity and their mobility. In the present economic situation, it will be increasingly difficult to make people believe that the labour market is difficult because workers lack the necessary qualifications.

9. Expose the silencing of union and political organizations evidenced by their inability to take up the previous points, alienated as they are by their collaboration with industrial firms for the purpose of strengthening the worker's status, thus helping to develop the myth of salvation through access to power of knowledge, thereby reinforcing the imperialism of the knowledge capitalists have over the industrialized masses. The right for which recognition should be obtained is the right not to take part in educational processes, that is, the right to satisfy one's own educational needs outside the educational machine.

If loss of earnings and rental values are brought into account as a part of the cost of this education, a country such as France already spends the equivalent of nearly a third of the total education budget on continuing vocational training, or in other words, on the industrialization of adults, the redeployment of the work force and the growth of human assets. In 1973 more than half of this sum was provided by the state from the budgets of various ministries, while the remainder was contributed directly by industry.

In that year more than two million workers, or 14 per cent of all employed workers as against 10 per cent in 1972, took vocational training courses. This estimate does not include the training courses in public service, or those attended by the self-employed.

Assuming that budgets remained at the same level, one could predict in 1973 that all workers would receive training every 10 years; by 1974, this had been reduced to every seven years. It is not much, but it is already too much, particularly if one bears in mind that almost 50 per cent of them will never have this training, so that those who are already best provided for will attend more frequently.

No one has succeeded in demonstrating the direct influence of training on productivity—strangely, the impact of training on productivity is measured by income increases. Increasing expenditure must, therefore, be justified by something else, and serve some other purpose : the inculcation of an ideology, for example, the sharpening of the desire for personal advancement, in fact the domestication of the working class to fit the industrial ethos.

There is still time to protest as long as the permanent education process has not engulfed the entire adult population. But in the United States the number of enrolments for part-time courses for adults is larger than that in full-time education institutions. In Sweden, about two million people above school age take part in part-time education, as against 1,500,000 pupils in the compulsory system. Even if the full-time equivalent is probably not more than 10 per cent of compulsory education, a first important threshold has been crossed. The cost must be counted.

The control of increasing budgets, like the power and prestige attached to teaching, is now passing from the teachers and their schools to the instructors and their multi-media systems, with a view to their obtaining an even more subtle and pervasive control of individuals.

The institutionalization of permanent education will transform society into an enormous planet-sized classroom watched over by a few satellites. Only the labels will enable one to distinguish it from an enormous hospital ward, from a planetary mental home and from a penitentiary universe, where education, punishment, medical care and imprisonment are synonymous. The industrial method of teaching will be replaced by an even more destructive post-industrial conditioning.

It is now urgent to open a public inquiry into the political, cultural and ethical costs of deschooled education. The poor countries are more able than the rich to choose to diversify opportunities of learning within the context of a shared way of life, through the proliferation of relevant personal experiences. The rich countries have few options open beyond those imposed on them by their industrial mega-machines—of education which has to be in continual growth the better to secure the bureaucratic control of mankind.

POLITICAL INVERSION

Ivan Illich

Individuals need tools to move and dwell. They need remedies for their diseases and resources to communicate with one another. Some of these things people cannot make for themselves. They depend on being supplied with objects and services which vary from culture to culture. Some people depend on the supply of shoes and others on the supply of ovens. Some need to get aspirins and others printing presses.

People do not need only to obtain things; they need above all the freedom to make things among which they can live, to give shape to them according to their own taste, and to put them to use in caring for and about others. Prisoners often have access to more things and services than other members of their families, but they have no say in how things are to be made and cannot decide what to do with them. Their punishment consists in being deprived of what I shall call conviviality.

I choose the term conviviality to designate the contrary of institutionalized productivity. I want it to mean autonomous and creative intercourse among persons, and intercourse of persons with their environment, and this in contrast with the conditioned response of persons to the demands made upon them by others or by their milieu. I consider conviviality individual freedom realized in mutual personal interdependence and, as such, an intrinsic ethical value. I believe that without conviviality life becomes meaningless and persons wither. I believe that as conviviality in any society is reduced below a certain level, no level of industrial productivity can effectively satisfy the needs of the members.

Present institutional purposes, hallowing productivity as they do at the expense of conviviality, are a major factor in the amorphousness and meaninglessness plaguing contemporary society. A schoolroom, a hospital, an urban intersection inCzechoslovakia can hardly be distinguished from one in the U.S. or Turkey or Argentina. Tie-ups on access-roads to a capital do not depend on the number of cars per one hundred inhabitants; they are as bad in Rio as they are on Long Island. Undoubtedly the central lane reserved for the party bureaucrats (and emergency vehicles) in Moscow will disappear under the onslaught of products from the new Fiat Factory in the Urals. And the more people in any society think that one must have a car, the less prone they are to take hitchhikers in their empty seats. Conviviality declines with rising productivity.

Since the mid-sixties everyone is beginning to be conscious of the way in which proliferation of goods is spoiling the physical environment. Rising productivity in the supply of manufactured goods has irreversible results in depletion and pollution, because the world's resources are limited and cannot support systems of production which make unlimited use of them. But the inevitable accumulation of durable junk in a constantly obsolescent society is so obvious that I do not want to labour it now.

Rather I intend to extend the concept of entropy. A school of thought is developing according to which the necessity of upper per capita limits in all areas of physical consumption can best be demonstrated by the evidence that world-wide production of energy must be held within certain parameters. On the order of magnitude of these parameters there might be considerable disagreement. (See the three fall issues of the *Bulletin of the Atomic Scientist.*) But most people would agree with the assistant director for energy and environment, Executive Office of President Nixon, that we will soon approach them. He says:

'The exhaustion of energy resources is not itself apt to be the crux of the problem. It is the impact on air, water and land in utilizing these tremendous volumes with present technology which is really troublesome, for the environmental and health and safety problems are present, no matter which forms of energy we examine . . . What seems to me dangerous is that the changes will be gradual and that man will adjust to more and more pollution in a synthetic environment cut off from any natural surroundings. As Rene Dubos has stated, perhaps the greater danger is that man will survive, but gradually lose much of his humaneness.'

What I do want to call attention to is a parallel process in the service sector: the fact that rising productivity and supply of services results in the irrecuperable loss of conviviality. It deprives persons of their own potency, of their freedom and society of the memory that these could once have been treasured.

This reversal of institutional purposes, i.e., from conviviality to productivity, is equally typical for societies where the producer is told that he is in the saddle. It is also used as a measurement of the level of development a society has achieved. Societies in which most people depend for most of their goods and services

26

on the personal whim, kindness or skill of another are called 'underdeveloped', while those in which living has been transformed into a process of ordering from an all-encompassing store-catalogue are called 'advanced'.

Every aspect of these advanced societies (be they capitalist, Marxist, or whatever) has become part of a larval system for escalating production and consumption that is necessary to justify and pay for it. The classical society of capitalist accumulation is being transformed into a consumer society. The very nature of consumption is in the process of change: intangible merchandise (such as information, education, health) is assuming an ever greater place in the march of progress and its cost rises even more rapidly than that of tangible merchandise (goods). Finally the ethic of conspicuous consumption gives way to the obsessive compulsion to produce insofar as the syndicates aspire to the ethic of the 'leisure mass'.[1]

For this reason, criticism of bad management, official dishonesty, and technological lag simply distract the public attention from the issue which counts. Equally distracting is the suggestion that productivity pursued under the tutelage of a planning board which protects the interests of a majority would lead to less frustrating results than productivity sky-rocketing under the pressure of dissatisfied consumers. Attempts to improve the quality of products, or the equity of their distribution, will only increase pollution, impotency, and overdetermination and rob not only the rich, but also the poor, of conviviality, which now is still their primary treasure.

The scientific challenge

The progress of science is frequently blamed for this functional shift of institutions from frameworks for action to factories of goods, a shift which in several European languages is reflected in a simultaneous linguistic shift from verb to substantive for the designation of their purpose. For example the activity of housing oneself is reduced to that of purchasing a home; the activity of educating children is reduced to their being given an 'education', (a term called 'vicious' by Voltaire); to go somewhere means to be seated in some mode of transportation.

No doubt it is true that scientific discoveries are now used to render supply-funnels for commodities more copious and allow them to crowd off the scene toolshops for independent enterprise. But all this is not the fault of scientific input in itself. It is rather the result of the intent with which science is applied. Science could be equally well used to increase the tool-kit available to every man, endowing individuals and transient gatherings of associates to constantly re-create their environment with undreamt of freedom and formerly unthinkable self-expression.

In 1945 30% of all houses in Massachusetts were owner-built, at least to some extent; today the figure is down to 19%. Certainly new materials and handy tools could have made possible an increase rather than a decline of housing as an activity expressed by those who want to dwell there.

The number of medicines and knowledge about their usefulness and their side-effects has grown immensely in the last two generations. Yet in the same time information about them has become increasingly restricted; even the Merck Manual is now inaccessible to the layman. Increasingly medicines are considered mysterious and dangerous unless prescribed by a doctor, who does his prescribing quite possibly over a phone.

Books have become cheaper to produce than they ever have been. Yet the number of books purchased yearly by a high school graduate in the U.S. has fallen constantly over the last two decades and is now lower than any comparably developed country. One should think that this would lead at least to the use of other educational devices outside of 'programs', be they offered in school or over TV. Instead the populace is so thoroughly trained to desire only what is packaged and channeled through a delivery hook-up that most of what all citizens know is acquired in audiences numbered by the millions when a station finds it profitable to program it.

I believe that we are now near the point at which frustration created by several of these institutions will become unbearable. This happens as the attempts to improve either the quality of the product or the equity with which they serve their clients proves futile. At this point the political atmosphere will be ripe to re-define the purpose which institutions should serve in a technological age. Present institutions provide clients with pre-determined goods. Desirable institutions ought to enable creative people to meet their own needs. Present institutions have made commodities out of health, education, housing, transportation, and welfare. We need arrangements which permit modern man to engage in the activities of healing and health maintenance, learning and teaching, moving and dwelling. I propose to set a legal limit to the tooling of society in such a way that the toolkit necessary to conviviality will be accessible for the autonomous use of a maximum number of people. In other words, we make conviviality the criterion for the level of productivity of society's tooling.

If science were thus used to increase the power of the indivi-dual to create his milieu and to care for each other, this would provide the leverage through which institutional purposes could be inverted. It would make it possible to substitute the question: 'What tools do people need and what do they have to know if they want to heal or if they want to care for those in the process of being healed?' for the current concern with the delivery of anonymous health services.

But such an inversion of institutional purposes cannot be the result of market pressure, nor can the managers of our industries who are used to wielding the power by which they provide people with commodities be expected to turn into switchboard managers of a market. The decision to limit the use of technology to increase productivity for the profit of industry and instead to increase the use of technology in a way which actually competes with and contradicts the ideals of an industrial society, this decision is the most important challenge for radical politics and legislation during the seventies. The translation of this social imperative into political terms can be clearly projected.

The political challenge

Politics is the formal structure and process by which a given society expresses and enforces the values it happens to accept. All present political systems, be they labelled liberal, Marxist, or conservative, express and enforce productivity at the expense of conviviality. They provide goods with clients rather than people with goods. Individuals are forced to pay for and use things they do not need; they are allowed no effective part in the process of choosing, let alone producing them. Products multiply for the sake of proliferation, which keeps the process of production expanding.

What I want to propose is a radically new politics, a politics that will enforce the individual's right to use only what he needs, to play an increasing part as an individual in its production, and to guarantee an environment so simple and transparent that all men most of the time have access to all the things which are useful to care for themselves and for others. Such politics would have as its major goal an inversion of present institutional purposes.

Just because I define politics as I do, I take it seriously. And I believe that very soon, as a result of the recognition of ·the frustration caused by present institutional purposes, the time will be ripe for a political restructuring of the relationship between production and consumption, certainly for the reverse of what Marx foresaw and hoped for in 1843: a society full of useful things and useless people. I look forward to a society, and so to a political structure, that will enable creative persons to meet their needs both as producers and as users.

As it is, it has become almost senseless to oppose the political left to the right. You cannot tell a liberal from a conservative unless he wears a button. The economists of socialist and capitalist countries do the same with different rhetoric. The public budget of rich and poor countries shows mainly quantitative differences. New politics has come to mean new ways of getting more of the same.

Present political platforms appeal to their following by proposing a set of goods and services the economy shall provide if and when the party gets into power. Each party presents a different profile of the minimum quanta it promises to provide for everybody. Each tailors its promises to the probable consensus of a particular group of voters. The political platform consists in promising every citizen to provide as a pedestal a jumble of tangible and intangible products which will permit him finally to live as a human being. By doing so politics becomes a process by which the voters agree on what is insufficient, leaving undetermined what amount of consumption of public resources shall be considered good enough, while not imposing any limits on what ought to be considered excessive, as long as its use by a person can somehow be justified as being for the common good.

The alternative to such a political platform would be one which offers a profile of upper limits on the resources which any individual may use either in his own or in the public interest, something which seems to be logically antecedent to the promise of a guaranteed minimum quantum for everybody. Such alternate politics would generate a consensus on what society considers enough for a person, and good enough for everybody over a long period of time. The guarantee of a foundation or base satisfactory to each depends on the imposition of a ceiling for all.

One clear example of the need for maximum limits and an obvious danger in their misapplication is seen in the already-mentioned area of pollution. The late sixties produced a vast amount of data on the threat to our physical environment. An excellent summary and selective bibliography can be found in **Garrett De Bell**, *The Environmental Handbook,* Ballantine Books, New York, 1970. Also **R.P. Sangster,** *Ecology: A Selected Bibliography,* Council of Planning Librarians Exchange Bibliography, No. 170. Much more important for my argument is a recent trend in literature on the subject, which shows how the arguments of conservationists are already used for politically conservative purposes. **James Ridgeway,** *Politics of Pollution* Dutton, New York, 1970 provides evidence of the U.S. government complicity with industry in exploiting public concern with pollution for anti-social purposes. **Richard Neuhaus,** *in Defense of People: Ecology and the Seduction of Radicalism* Macmillan, New York, 1971 elaborates on an important theme: the myth of ecology as a non-partisan and apolitical rallying point for all men of good will, which threatens to short-circuit the political process and leaves the present power brokers with more authority than ever to direct national destinies. I consider Neuhaus' warning central to our theme. Pollution increases and its destructive effects become more visible. Fear of further pollution can become a new demagogic tool to deny the large masses (who are minimal consumers) any further rise in their standards of consumption, while providing increased power for technocrats, which they will need to keep the poor in their place. But I also believe that the evidence of rising pollution can serve to rally an enormous majority of people to a political platform which would set upper limits for per-capita consumption and pollution, limits which would seriously reduce present living standards for a minority, and which would be for most people now alive far beyond their wildest dreams.

Our political imagination is now challenged to find a process by which a commitment to personal austerity, to voluntary poverty, can be translated into democratically enforceable programs. Unfortunately since the time of Stalin it has become difficult to claim the socialist label for such politics.

In February of 1931 the U.S. depression hit bottom, Trotsky and Buckarin had been defeated and Stalin launched the USSR on the road of ruthless industrialization. He gave the reason why: 'We are 50 or 100 years behind the advanced countries. We must make good the lag in 10 years.'

Stalin translated 'the control over the means of production' to mean the increase of productivity by new means used for the control of the producer. Since then, a socialist policy is one which serves the productivity of a socialist country.

Stalin's interpretation of this fundamental Marxist goal has since then served as a form of blackmail against socialists and the left. This can be clearly seen in relation to formerly colonial countries, to which Lenin assigned a 'revolutionary' role. Stalin's principle permits the interpretation of whatever increases the amount of schooling, the increase of the road system, and the productivity of extraction and manufacture as revolutionary. To be on the left has come to mean either to champion the nation which lags in production or to help the minority which lags in consumption to catch up.

The rebirth of a meaningful left, both national and inter-

32

national, depends on the ability to learn to distinguish the control of the means and of the mode of production in the service of people from the control of people for the purpose of raising output at all cost and then worrying how to distribute it in a fair way. New technologies have rendered production so powerful that social control of benefits is illusory unless it extends to the control of 'what' is industrially produced and 'if' it is needed. Such a social inversion of goals, if it is successfully expressed in a political formulation of maxima rather than minima, will demand a comparable inversion of the major institutions of society: education, health-care, transportation, housing, etc.

I hope to deal in subsequent pages with a variety of reasons for which it has become difficult to make political proposals aimed at the self-limitation of technology as the basic condition for the creation of a new left. The main reason is that our political imagination is mesmerized by alternatives for the production of more things for more people and thus is paralyzed when we try to focus on a possible inversion of this political goal. New and radical politics means to make the need for upper limits of per-capita consumption into the center of our world-wide aspirations, in order to plan a technology for man's use which replaces the present technology which subordinates human needs to ever increasing productivity.

The task of institutional inversion

There are strategic reasons for choosing 'de-schooling' as the first step in a more general program of institutional inversion. Most people have school behind them. The world's majority knows that it has been irremediably excluded from satisfactory schooling. Others who did go through a 'good' school know that they have been hurt in the process. And finally most who were benefitted in some way by school know that they did not learn in school what helped them to do their job, and also that whatever school contributed to their success was probably not the subject matter they were taught. Agreement on the need to disestablish schools can be reached.[3]

In previous articles written for the *New York Review of Books*. I have shown that education based on *output* of a school system is bound to fail. Inevitably the economic costs of such education grow faster than the GNP which they are supposed to boost. This is true for all countries, rich and poor, during the sixties. Quantifiable education produced by schools serves as a rationale to correlate productivity and income on a world-wide basis. Inevitably also a society which defines education as a commodity discourages learning from participation in everyday life and creates a rationale for an environment in which fewer people have access to the facts and tools that shape their lives. This is so because information becomes shrouded in a secrecy which dissolves only for those who pass through an appropriate graded ritual of initiation, and because tools are made scarce and reserved to the few to whom information is reserved, supposedly for the purpose of making their products plentiful. In summary, I have shown that schools, by creating a hierarchy of knowledge-capitalists, whether the particular society considers itself socialist or not, alienates men from other men by reducing interaction in the relationships between professionals and their clients, and also alienate man from his environment by making the consumer into a marginal participant in the processes by which his needs are satisfied. In these articles I hope also to have shown that the translation of education into the process of accumulating certified shares of the knowledge stock serves to rationalize access to the scarce upper levels of a consumer society and to justify a technocratic organization which each year produces more expensive and therefore scarcer goods, which in turn are reserved primarily for the knowledge capitalists who hold a high rank in the technocracy.

I have argued that the present crisis in education will only be accentuated by a further increase in the output of schools. I am not surprised that since then we have obtained considerable evidence that the crisis which I described principally in the forms in which it now appears in the U.S. on the one side and in poor countries on the other has moved to the center of attention also in countries whose GNE (Gross National Education) lies between these two.

The crisis in education can be solved only through an inversion of the institutional structure of agencies which now serve it. It can be overcome only if the present schools, with or without walls, which prepare or authorize programs for students are replaced by new institutions which are more like libraries and matching services and which empower the learner to find access to the tools and the encounters which he needs to learn to fit his own choices.

Schools enable a teacher to establish classes of subjects and to impute the need for them to classes of people called pupils.the inverse of schools would be opportunity networks which permit individuals to state their present interest and seek a match for it.

It is relatively easier for an adult to imagine a world without schools, however, than it is for him to foreswear the need of a hospital, but to do the first might lead to the second. **It is evident that the structural inversion of our major institutions will either happen for several of them more or less together or it will not happen at all.** It cannot happen as long as people have not become aware of the illusion which modern economics foster. Once the veil of illusion has been thrown aside, all major institutions as at present constituted become vulnerable. As the school is already undergoing inversion, possibly the health services monolith is next most accessible, with transportation and housing becoming open to attack at the same time.

The application of such an inversion of social goals through the politics of maximum rather than minimum limits would, as I shall develop further, find its expression through the inversion of the structure of the institutions which now deliver to us education, health, welfare, or other goods.

Schools, hospitals, and armies not only look alike everywhere in the world; the economic reasoning underlying their planning as well comes only in different shades of the same color. Nixon's advisors differ from those appointed by Brezhnev, Franco, and unfortunately also Castro, mostly in that they are less candid in the statement of their metaphysics.

Economists provide us with the axiom on which all their

35

reasoning is based. This axiom states that frustration is the inevitable outcome of satisfaction and that there cannot be enough of a good thing but only more. The Council of Economic Advisors in this year's report to the President sum up the reason why: 'If it is agreed that economic output is a good thing, it follows by definition that there is not enough of it.' In this view man is a bottomless trashcan, an incurable consumer and a compulsive producer. Productive institutions have the sole purpose of providing him with operant conditioning for the escalating exploitation which guarantees their further growth.[4]

The C.E.A. acknowledges that there might be a limit to the ills growth could cure. 'The growth of GNP has its costs and beyond some point these are not worth paying.' But the C.E.A. does not waste any effort toward determining this point. In fact growth-economics provides no method of pinpointing the level at which planned costs outgrow planned benefits, since both are subsumed under the same category of 'institutional outputs.' Therefore all the Council does is to state that further growth cannot be stopped. 'The existing propensities of the population and the policies of the government constitute claims upon GNP itself that can only be met by rapid economic growth.' The C.E.A. declares itself incompetent either to challenge the de-facto dictatorship of the consumer or to change the policies enacted by those industrial managers whom the consumer has selected to exercise his dictatorship.

Western economists explain the need for open-ended growth as the consensus of the unlimited wants of consumers, which the party wanting to stay in power has to meet. Socialist economists explain the same need for unlimited growth as the manifestation of historical progress. In fact the advancement of the society to higher forms of production is used to justify the dictatorship of a victorious proletariat which the party officials represent. They presume to dictate higher production for its own sake, rather than for the presumed satisfaction of their constituency.

The Western economist speaks in the name of Ford and Ford's captive consumer-mass. The growth maniac socialist speaks in the name of a producer-class and advocates that this class aspire to become as soon as possible its own most exploited client. Both seem to agree on one point: the fundamental historical evolution is that of technology, which involves a growth of productivity as irreversible as it is irresistible.

Insurance:
the market as
a gamble

As already mentioned, modern nations tend to look alike and this in at least three ways: they use identical tools; they use the same toolkit; and they use the same methods to distribute their outputs. Schools are tools to produce education; hospitals are tools to produce health-services; and mass-circulation papers or programs the tools to provide daily information. These tools depend on each other. The growth of the medical profession depends on the output level of medical schools, just as the number of medical schools depends on the availability of teaching hospitals. Finally access to the more costly services of both hospitals and schools depends on some form of legalized gamble. The medical profession, its place among other professions, and the lottery which gives access to its service differ from country to country only in name and in niceties, like flags differ from each other.

Under Johnson, a religious war about the name of the medical gamble came to an end in the US. Americans agreed to call their distribution system henceforth an 'insurance plan'. Since then different model plans were designed and they are now proposed to the public that it may choose one of them as a monopoly. Whichever model wins, the benefit accrues to the medical profession. Politics thus has become the art of playing on the same set of instruments the tune which each party hopes will bewitch the majority. The 1972 elections might become the first in history staked on a popularity contest between two publicity campaigns both organized to provide a monopoly for the same industrial complex called 'health'.[5]

It is of the nature of a national health insurance to channel tax resources for spending under the control of doctors. It is equally in its nature to re-enforce the idea that the doctor's services are priceless, and also that he alone ought to decide how much of them is desirable for each patient.

Compulsory health insurance is the first step towards compulsory health treatment. Until now the citizen was just considered immoral if he did not play at a lottery called health insurance with an open drawing date. In the new game he must play — and the doctor's house must win.

When medical insurance becomes obligatory and provides access to potentially unlimited treatment, should professional reasons make it desirable, it becomes a regressive tax. Those who die quickest get the least service, and those who die slowly get the most questionable service. Medical costs per capita rise steeply as death approaches. Doctors and their institutions are encouraged to concentrate their services on the clinical consolation of the dying. Insurance provides the medical profession with more resources for life-prolongation, drawn from a society which becomes less healthy in the process of producing them. Compulsory health insurance thus opens the door for unending extortion by the medical profession.[6]

All this, of course, is true only as long as no upper limit is set on the per capita outlay of public expenditure. Public control of the medical complex stands and falls with the honesty with which the need for such a limit is faced. Lay boards with the power to hire or fire doctors and set their maximum fees do control individual dishonesty; they cannot curb the hubris of a doctor who considers the death of a patient after a serious cancer operation as a defeat of his profession. If doctors trained with public resources and treatments provided from tax-funds were restricted to the use on their own recognizances of a limited set of treatments, the public could control the medical industry. Without facing this decision, the discussion of alternate insurance plans which guarantee everybody a minimum and also, but only if the doctor wants it, the infinite, is meaningless.

38

As things stand, health insurance guarantees services of unknown quality and quantity. It is advertised as a way to provide individuals with more power over their own destiny. In fact it provides them with as much choice among certified professionals as they have among politicians when they go to vote. At best an insurance gives the insured the choice to commit himself and his destiny to the intake officer in the medical complex. It remains with the doctor to determine the mix of consumer goods which will be packaged for the service of his patient. The doctor sets the tune at which hospitals, drugs, psychotherapy, and if necessary, the straight jacket will be orchestrated for the consumption of the beneficiary. What he shall get will be determined for him when somebody else decides the time to do so has come.

This cannot be changed as long as the insurance scheme is set up to deliver the output of a growth-industry to a client; its outputs *by definition* are scarce.

The doctor like the economist is dedicated to the principle that medical services are good and therefore by definition, always insufficient. His traditional ethics will tell him that he should leave nothing undone for the patient. Hundreds of years ago this meant a nightwatch at his bedside. Today it might mean the transfer of a terminal cancer patient from the operating room to the intensive care unit. There the doctor can pump resources into a dying body to force it to survive his tour of duty. The doctor becomes a sinister copy of the economist bent on all-purpose growth at all costs, especially if this can postpone collapse until after the next man takes over. If the patient resists the physician's care, he calls his psychiatric colleague to help him overcome such terminal consumer resistance.

Individual doctors will condemn this caricature of a healer who has transformed himself into an artist of maximum torture through optimum treatment. They do know that regular sleep, a balanced diet, and no smoking would add many more years to the life of each of their patients than all the services they can provide. But personal modesty and common sense cannot free the doctor from the dynamics of an institutional complex which shapes his environment and that of his client. The monopoly of hospitals over the care of people who have to stay in bed is reflected in the architecture of modern homes. It has become unfeasible to be sick at home, and embarrassing to stay there waiting for death.[7]

The fact remains that under the pressure of the health professions the maintenance of health, assistance in the restoration of health after an accident or during a crisis, and finally terminal life-prolongation have been monopolized by one industry, somewhat in the manner in which age-specific custodial care, certification, social initiation and instruction were packaged together by schools. In this process the length of time during which a person remains a patient or actual client of the doctor by staying alive has become the most significant measurable dimension of health. Life expectancy has become the most cherished proof of the increase of health in a population, even though its increase has little or nothing to do with the intake of medical services, except among the dying.

As a result of all this, an ageing population has come to translate 'health' into a life-prolonging commodity. A population thus fed on statistics has transformed ageing into the consumption of a lengthening life-expectancy which can be achieved by drinking of the medical fountain of geriatrics. Even the best of doctors, however, will find it difficult to avoid his patient's lumping together under the designation 'medical care' the declining relief he can offer and the growing pain and frustration which he can provide.

In the United States the outlay for health services increased in a few years by 12%, higher than the inflation in all other sectors. The increase in favor of the first years of life is even more marked and that for illnesses in the last two years of life the most exorbitant of all. I do not know of any study which reveals by what factor it would be necessary to multiply the medical output for men over 45 in 1900 to arrive at the sum spent today on their treatment and hospitalization. But census information indicates that the life expectancy of a 45 year old man in the U.S.A. in 1900 was 24.8 years more. In 1968 the life expectation of a man of the same age was 27.5 years. The probability that they spend those added weeks in hospitals, asylums, or homes for the aged has also increased disproportionately.

A society which defines medicine as the art of life-extension deserves to be governed by economists who define themselves as the architects of sustained and unlimited growth. Both the medical and the economic enterprise thus conceived are the out-growth of an illusion from which people suffer who deny the human need for upper limits because they are compelled to evade the necessity of facing death. A swelling GNP is the proper idol for people who demand from their doctors not to help them to heal but to keep them alive. It is the ultimate symbol of value in a society which defines its growing anxiety in terms of its bur-geoning wealth. Belief in the value of the GNP provides the final solution to the troublesome challenge, i.e. the need to measure benefits in a culture in which all that is desirable can somehow be reduced to wealth.

Psychologically growth economics cannot be separated from a medicine which finds its principle achievements in the avoidance of death. GNP is a concept homologous with life expectancy. It represents that grand total of the market value of all benefits plus the expenditures incurred to protect society from the unwanted side effects which result from the production of these benefits. A rising GNP gages the state of a nation as medical bills do the health of a man.

The doctor is trained to provide increasing pains at increasing cost, just as the economist stimulates increasing demand to produce increasing sales. Dr. Mendelsohn estimates that 90% of Chicago's outlay for public and private medicine and for treat-ment of clients actually increases suffering rather than healing or soothing it.

Reactionary 'modernization': two versions

The economist does literally provide for our society the abstract definition of its original sin, just as metaphysicians and theologians provided it for other times. The economist formulates the anthropology which fits our society in the most abstract terms, and defines man as a being who finds happiness in paying the highest possible price for his own operant conditioning to escalating frustration. Institutional output thus becomes the 'good' because in Walden III by definition consumers *want* to increase the frustration they can obtain from it.

In many areas of everyday life, as already noted, frustration grows faster than habituation to it. In some cases frustration has already reached a critical point. A wave of dissatisfaction with schools swept over some countries in the late sixties. This led the U.S. to the establishment of some ten thousand alternative educational centers. In Peru it led to the first legal attempt to disestablish schools and prohibit any discrimination based on previous school attendance. Analagous waves of sudden disenchantment with industrial complexes less sacred than school will be rising during the next few years.

There are already indications that the frustration of the public is reaching the critical level with the institutions that produce health, transportation, food-processing, and housing. But so long as that frustration re-enforces the dependance of our society on the unrestrained pursuit of the utmost institutional output, considered as a panacea, the remedy will produce onlydeception.[8]

In the perspective in which I here envisage our society, the 'technological solutions' and the 'politico-economic' solutions, which are generally opposed to each other, are seen as two complementary props of unlimited growth. It makes no difference that the control of the quality of merchandise be the result of organized consumer pressure directed by a student of Ralph Nader or that the same amelioration be the result of a humanitarian decision of a puritan bureau-technocrat. And what is even more decisive, it makes little difference if the transition from the organization of private services toward that of public services be done under the impulsion of technocrats or of idealogues. For example, the passing of the era of the private car and even of transportation by individual vehicle is probably very close for reasons of economy, efficacy and ecology. It is of little importance to my argument whether public transportation more rapid still, be established by the conspiracy of an international capitalist conglomerate or by political principle.

I hope I will be understood, therefore, if I choose as a model of those who fight for more satisfactory consumption certain students of Ralph Nader and, on the other hand, as models of those who struggle for more rational production Mr. Buckminster Fuller.[9]

These advocates of modernization as the remedy for the crisis in our institutions take two distinct reactionary roads. Each claims to lead through a revolution, and each in fact support the *modus quo*. Each of these so-called revolutions shifts the blame for the dysfunction of our institutions onto a different scape-goat and neither indicts the institutional purpose itself. The first so-called revolution speaks for the consumer, and blames the price and the quality of commodities on the manufacturer. Its proponents would like to take over Ford's department of design and of pricing. The promoters of the second, the scientific or technological revolution go a step further, to a point of myth-making that justifies calling their proposals 'technosophic'. They want, for instance, to achieve a breakthrough in the entire trans-portation industry which would provide them with more speed, and they do not care if they get it with or without cars. In more general terms, they propose to make our institutions serve their present ultimate purposes by providing them with more powerful tools.

I will show that each of these two revolutions advocates a more thorough espousal of our present world view, in which our needs can be satisfied only by tangible or intangible commodities which we consume. Each of the two movements provides new legitimacy for the present mode of production which I have already described · as operational re-enforcement of the consumer's willingness to accept rising hardship for diminishing, though more ardently pursued, satisfaction.

First, 'Naderism'[10] or the counter-revolution of the consumer. Cars are costly. They are unsafe. They do pollute. It is easy to blame the car manufacturer for the high price, the unreliable per-formance, and the unchecked side-effects. It is expedient to organize frustrated consumers, even though at first this is dangerous, as Nader had to learn, and ultimately futile.

Disciplined addicts can force the Mafia to peddle pure drugs. They cannot blame the junkey for selling a narcotic. The leader of the consumer revolt of the future might ride to the presidency on the prototype of a durable, non-polluting family plane. I imagine that he will smoke ten filter cigarettes and advocate a 'pure drug law' applicable to all commodities. He will campaign on the platform that the way to have your cake and eat it too is to make it grow not only bigger but also sweeter.

If the manufacturers of cars, of medical services, or of professional teaching were enlightened in their self-interest, they would support such a crusade which does their consumer research for them. Ownership of a car does guarantee the right to move. If the roads are good, it guarantees the right to move fast. But this is no more guarantee for good locomotion than access to a hospital is a guarantee for medical care. Just as in the case of health, more goods can mean less benefits. The higher the speed at which a man habitually moves, the greater today the amount of time he uses to get from one place to another. In 1948 the Interstate Highway system opened for traffic. Since then the percentage of vehicles travelling faster than 60 mph. on all main rural roads in the U.S.A. has tripled from 16 to 45 per cent. The time spent by each American in a car has grown and his time spent on the go by other means has increased even more. The maximum speed occasionally available to the member of a society is an indicator of the amount of time spent travelling. Americans spend more time travelling than Poles, and Poles spend more time travelling than Brazilians, just as a member of the jet set spends more time away from home than an ordinary citizen. Cheaper, safer, and non-polluting cars travelling on wider and straighter roads at higher speeds would enable their owners to spend more time safely packaged up on the go. Ford can be blamed for undesirable cars and then will produce desirable cars. Ford cannot be blamed for the fact that the increased output of cars increases the distresses of transportation.

The technosophic counterrevolution can be called the Buckminster Fuller syndrome, whose exponents blame the distressing nature of transportation on a conspiracy between Mr. Ford and his clients. They rightly claim that this unholy alliance for mutual exploitation keeps cars on the road and builds more roads with the tax-payer's money. These technosophs would like to do away with cars in order to improve transportation. For instance, they would like to see 'future gravitrains falling of their own weight along underground channels and then swooping up again on a combination of their own momentum and pneumatic air . . . all of which would be practical with the development of cheap laser tunneling'. This idea comes from the Secretary of Transportation of the U.S.A., Mr. Volpe. Proposals for public transportation, while discrediting the car, support the commitment of the society to provide more speed at all cost.

Some technosophs are simple technocrats; they are all the men on duty in Washington and Moscow. They provide their employers with more power or profits and maintain their legitimacy by claiming that this power is used to serve the majority.

Others describe themselves as the prophets of a man-made paradise; these call themselves techno-anarchists. They have fallen victim to the illusion that it is possible to socialize the technocratic imperative. They would make their followers believe that the maximum technically possible is not simply the maximum desirable for a few, but that it can also provide everybody with maximum benefits at minimum cost. Of course this is true, but only if the client wants the specific thing the technosoph tells him he wants.

The spokesmen for the consumer and the technosoph are both reactionary, but the latter more profoundly so. A consumer revolution succeeds if the consumer gets what he needs from the shelf of a supermarket, from the docket of a court, or from the catalogue of a university. Its success is the result of a conspiracy between salesmen and customer to provide good air-conditioners, useful degrees, and properly labelled drugs and to control the shareholder or aparatchik. As durable junk accumulates in and out of use, the consumer still maintains real options. People may prefer clean air while bicycling to work and avoid highways on which survival depends on air-conditioning. Employers may accept competence acquired in apprenticeship in lieu of certificates proving assistance at classes. Organized consumers, students, or welfare recipients provide a messy, though effective support for a chaotic, but powerful production system. The legal recognition of their sundry demands re-enforces the legal protection of the producers. The consumer can have a kind of victory, then, although it is only a temporary one.

'Technosophic' solutions deprive the consumer of even that chance. I recently attended a meeting in which the utilization of satellites for diagnostic ends was discussed. In the not too distant future we will be able to transmit the clinical data of a patient from any phone in Latin America to a system of central information and obtain in response diagnostic indications. Before receiving these, supplementary information must be obtained about the quantity of money available for the treatment, of little consequence whether it comes from public or private resources.

Any political success of a technosophic establishment, therefore, represents a step forward into a world where basic choices are fewer. Such a success is always a result of a collusion between government and an industrial complex; a conspiracy between a particular group of consumers and a particular industry is not sufficient to support its cost.

Whenever a technosophic 'solution' is adopted, this means that the party in power has committed the nation far beyond its mandate to govern, and that it has decided on what shall be made feasible on the advice of some scientific group holding secret knowledge of what is possible at an escalating cost. The adoption of a technological 'solution' means a political commitment without recourse to vote.

Once minimum speed is guaranteed to commuters, each person could be forced to use it, whether he likes it or not, as witness the minimum allowable speed now on many highways. The pattern which urbanization would take would impose the demand, without the need of a new breed of officers pressing truant commuters into a train. From now on, each victory for a new 'system' will be equivalent to a move towards a society in which each man is encapsuled in multiple compulsory insurance of his consumption. The government would make sure that he gets the speed, housing, medical care, or constant re-schooling experts need to progress. Each of these steps will require another enormous investment borrowed from the future and would amount to a new re-enforcement of our present mode of production. This, of course, goes far beyond simple consumer protection; it means mandatory consumption and addiction to the straight stuff, with only the freedom left to take more, not less.

To go from the present transportation-maze to gravitrains, or from our school-system to life-long re-education, or from the clinical labs to the diagnostic satellite follows the same logic as progress from bombers to MIRV. To start developing the prototype is already a political decision, costly, monopolistic, and irreversible. It is also an overkill of problems now created by our institutions. Just as the use of MIRV guarantees for everybody equally effective extinction (not safety), so would life-long re-education provide everybody with constant re-assignment to his place in a meritocracy, and speedier transportation would compel everybody to longer trips, shorter stays, and no way to get somewhere with his feet.

The technosoph promises to increase the output of our institutions by eliminating their current product; he provides transportation at a higher speed and for everybody. But this transportation is 'better' only for those clients who let the new system translate being 'better' mean being as much as possible on the move at the highest feasible speed, rather than being at rest somewhere.

What the guarantee of minima means can best be illustrated by looking again at the oldest profession first entrusted with offering a minimum. Once the graduates of teachers' colleges were given a public monopoly to decide what constitutes good education, they had to use it to disqualify learning which happened outside their control. Schools became the only legitimate recipients for public funds destined for education. Inevitably learning was translated into 'education', and this in turn became a commodity which could be obtained only from accredited schools. The guarantee of a minimum education was translated into the obligation to attend a minimum number of years. Soon dropouts, forced into the nether world destined for the so-called a-social, would be denied jobs. But the guarantee does not work only against him who does not use it. The monopoly of schools over education made education into an intangible commodity. It turned the result of learning into an invisible software, which is guaranteed by the code number given on the certificate. Those pupils who obtain only the legal minimum find out that they wasted their time in school: what they acquired is devalued on the market because others have more or a newer program.

Schools were not originally created with the intent of creating an industrial complex for the production of knowledge; they were meant to give everybody a chance to learn. But they became a form of compulsory insurance of every child's future productivity. The governments of the world all established the monopoly of a profession, giving them the right to decide how much of their expert treatment each citizen should get. Soon the profession could also decide how much of its treatment a concrete individual needed, and finally it could use its power to give it to him or to her. 'Insurance' of minimum requirements of any service is always a form of social control which permits the manager to manipulate economic flow by determining the level of that minimum. Universal insurance thus is a way of using the gambling instinct of a population to make compulsory consumption attractive.

Nader and Fuller only re-enforce what we now have. They do so on three matching levels. Their converging demands re-enforce the purpose of politics, strengthen the legitimacy of further professional specialization, and by this double support cement the industrial shape of all our institutions. They heighten the demand for insurance for all, for more specialized doctors or school teachers and unlimited delivery of healthcare services or educational software.

First, both of them support the appeal the politician now uses: the promise of a classless society made up of a luxury class with cake for all, and the moon, too, for those who reach out for it. Second, both Nader and Fuller play into the hand of the professions who alone know the secret formula necessary to accomplish this magic: the formula needed for the miraculous multiplication of cakes and the formula needed to satisfy everyone with cake and a vicarious moonwalk in exchange for this freedom to do each what he wants. And finally, the consumer-defender and the spokesman of unlimited production both build an airtight shell for our present world view according to which the mere fact of scientific advancement renders a trend irreversible which transforms all community enterprise into industries evaluated by measuring their outputs.

Both Nader and Fuller suggest that output could be an even better thing than it is today, and I cannot see what else this would mean but that there would be even less 'enough' of it.

The politics of conviviality

I have shown that economists spell out the metaphysics on the basis of which contemporary men are willing to agree. Political parties have built on this seeming evidence the economists provide. They have become publicity firms for the same cornucopia and they compete for the right to use their banners and slogans to shove it down the throat of their client. On a world-wide scale, capitalists and communists share the crypto-Stalinist fallacy. Major powers try to impose on each other their particular way of insuring minimum consumption levels for the masses. So powerfully has Stalinism corrupted our social imagination that we cannot conceive that an alternate institutional structure could be used in a technological society.

Our present technocopia is à society in which specialized producers monopolize the purpose of all major institutions, and growing productivity justifies their growing power. A political left, to be meaningful, would have to forego the various attempts to render our present institutions viable. It would have to focus on the task of inverting their trends towards rising productivity which renders conviviality dysfunctional. A hospital now has the purpose of providing the sick with professional and paraprofessional services and of excluding any relative, girl friend, or child who would want to care for and about his sick neighbor. Tolerable institutions would be those in which the productive and the convivial purpose temper each other. Such would be health centers from which sick having a neighbor could be well cared for at home. The concerned friend could find the tools to care better for them and perhaps someone to show them how to use those tools.

Our present institutions are high-pressure productions funnels which by their very structure contribute to the proliferation of increasing levels of subordinate professions and paraprofessions. Desirable institutions would by their very structure make it encumbent upon their managers to enable non-specialists to teach, to heal, to move, or to house each other in the hope that people who once have been engaged in any of these specialized activities will soon initiate others to the role provisionally still in the hand of a specialist.

For example, such institutions might well preclude certain types of brain surgery. At a recent meeting I overheard a group of neuro-surgeons make a surprising statement. They agreed that most of those special techniques by which they could contribute to healing and for which operating rooms could in fairness be provided in Latin America could be taught to a responsible peasant girl with a steady hand and intelligence in a matter of months. I repeated this statement to a group which included another doctor, a psychiatrist, and a neuro-surgeon. The last mentioned contradicted his colleagues, called them irresponsible. For the time being I accepted his correction. But later in the evening, this same man privately explained to me why some neuro-surgeons make irresponsible statements. He said that his was a frequently frustrating profession, that sometimes looking back on a week's work of several multi-hour operations, one had to admit that practically all his patients had died, and that, of those who survived the intervention, few would be able to live everyday lives. We parted as friends, he agreeing with me that at least in Latin America, and for the moment, medical resources could well be spent in an alternate way.

Convivial institutions providing tools which non-specialists can learn to use when the need for them arises inevitably impose limits on the tools which fit this purpose. It is quite easy to paint a scenario of alternate toolkits which would fit most of the needs of countries in which the majority of people needing tonsillectomies, bone setting, or appendectomies cannot now get them. It is less easy to render restrictions on the medical toolkit plausible to citizens of countries which have access to high technology.[11] One of the reasons for this difficulty is that most people are not aware of the cost they now pay in health-destruction in order to be allowed the high levels of health-service intake which they now 'enjoy'.

On this point it is significant that 70% of all advanced medicines which came onto the U.S. market in the period between 1945 and 1970 were again withdrawn from the market at the time the seventeen year patent protection had run out, and it had ceased to be in the interest of the manufacturer to push the product at all cost. Some might have been purposely withdrawn because the manufacturer wanted to push a new, more expensive product for which he could again claim mysterious qualities and a monopoly over another seventeen year period.

The marketing of tranquilizers by Hoffman-La Roche is a good example. First La Roche brought Librium onto the market. Just before patent-protection ran out, the almost equivalent Valium was intensely advertised as an advanced and more sophisticated product. In bulk the production cost per kg. is near $100. Packaging in 5 to 10 mg. doses of this weight might cost about $800. The marketing price in Canada is nearly $13,000. Now Valium is being replaced in the La Roche publicity by Nobrium, advertised as a cure-all for anxiety associated with almost any sickness. Evidence is lacking that any of these drugs, in the cases *where their use is indicated,* is superior to the cheap generics such as barbiturates. (See article by **Peter Burich** in *Guardian Weekly,* June 26th 1971.)

But much more frequently an item is withdrawn because at best it has not proven superior to a centuries-old cure and, at worst, its side-effects were by then amply documented and rendered further sales impossible. If Americans, Germans, and Frenchmen understood that they serve as human guinea pigs for extended testing of medicines which are still too expensive for the majority of poor people, they might awaken to the advantages the limitation on the pharmacopia might mean for them.

In its present production-oriented structure, medical care

51

translates into longer survival for a few, notwithstanding a biosphere which is corrupted by doctors, geneticists, and the factories which produce medical supplies. And for the majority in rich countries, medical dispensations serve the purpose for which Coca is used in lieu of salaries by the mine-owners of Bolivia: as a drug which keeps the Indian going deeper into the pits and happily unaware of his hunger.

The present structure of medical institutions is built on the concept of indefinite backup and referral, by which both economic and human costs are escalated out of sight. Most alternate schemes for the delivery of medical services are nothing but rearrangements of backup agencies. Some want neighborhood health-centers in which para-professionals can set bones, others arrangements by which the layman can do it, but all want a hierarchy of places to which a sick man can be transferred (with or without the company of an advocate from his neighborhood) so that nothing which science considers feasible might be left undone for his sake.

Radically reasonable politics would seek broad popular agreement on what medical care ought to be considered good enough. Without such an agreement, there is no way to insure a re-organized health-care system against being as impersonal as what we have, even though under a new name.

The fact that limits must be set on the amount of medical services available per capita is clear, if for no other reason than in order not to impose on the doctor the duty in each case of determining when the patient is allowed to die. How such limits are to be set, and how the measurement of the height of the ceiling ought to be achieved is less clear.[12]

How one could reach political agreement on an upper limit can better be illustrated in the case of the speed at which a society agrees locomotion of persons is fast enough, not only for commuters but equally for ambulances, policemen, and the campaigning politicians as well.

At present the search for open-ended speed has made of vehicles a second type of luxury home for a minority. As I have indicated, this same open-endedness of speed forces the majority of people in a 'mobile' society to switch from fixed to moving cages several times a day. In this process, the act of 'dwelling' becomes a luxury.

It ought to be possible to determine a level of speed at which most people compelled to use vehicles will spend least time in movement (which is something different from cruising), while depletion, pollution, and destruction of health are kept to a minimum. The search for such a level has to start from the insight into the present structure of transportation. The time spent moving, as I have shown, increases with the consumption of speed by a society while, at the same time, locomotion between two points, both of which are desirable, becomes the privilege of fewer and fewer people. Commitment to more speed blinds us to the obvious. Such escalation only further increases time spent commuting at rising levels of pollution, depletion, and unhealthy living.

The optimum level of speed would be a compromise between minimum time spent daily moving between equally attractive home and work places at minimum levels of pollution and with the maximum choice, at minimum personal cost, and abstention from the use of mechanical transportation altogether. A truly radical political platform which presents its voters with a well-reasoned choice of one among various possible profiles of upper limits for consumption should certainly contain such a speed limit.

The first reaction I get when discussing this matter with people who in principle follow my argument is that such an upper limit would have to be developed by experts. I doubt that this is true. Some very simple considerations will show that this speed limit within metropolitan areas would be somewhere in the order of 15 or 20 miles per hour. If people living in any of the major U.S. metropolitan areas were guaranteed effective locomotion permitting them to cover 15 miles in any given hour from any point to any point, they would be moving faster and better than they are now. We know that this could be achieved by banning private cars from the streets of New York, and that the saving in taxes which could result would make it possible for the city to provide transportation at minimum prices.

Searching for the coincidence of an optimum and a maximum

53

speed for two states of Mexico, both poor, rural, and with difficult terrain, to our great surprise we arrived at figures not significantly different from those which would meet the same criteria in New York. Surprising at first, this result indicates that technological dimensions which fit simultaneously the three criteria of ecological 'cleanliness', sociological 'fairness', and psychological 'desirability' are within a human rather than a cosmic range.

In the state of Chiapas live 1¼ million persons. During the last year not more than 10,000, which means less than 1% of them moved more than once during the year over a distance of twelve miles in the period of one hour. During each of the last thirty-five years, a sum of money was spent constructing roads for heavy vehicles, cars, and gasoline, with only a part of which it would be possible to provide 80% of all villages with access-trails and a supply of mechanical mules so ample that it would be practically unlimited. These simple vehicles powered by 2 HP motors capable also of driving dynamos, pumps, and plows could be built profitably within the state and made in a highly repair-intensive, durable form. Of course, this would mean a political decision to prescribe speeds above 12 miles per hour and to avoid all further expenditure for building an infrastructure for those few who now occasionally engage in such consumption.

The setting of upper limits on certain dimensions is not only necessary (as in the case of medical services) and can be discussed in quantitative terms (as I have shown in the case of speeds of locomotion). It is also the only way of providing the majority with what they need to survive.

John Turner shows clearly that the present attempt of the Mexican government to produce desirable housing by minimum standards has created an unbearable crisis in housing. By government regulation, the minimum house built according to minimum criteria set by the government costs seven annual incomes of an average wage earner, or the median monthly income if the house be rented rather than built. Such standards render it impossible for between 50% and 80% of the population already 'living' in Mexico City to 'dwell' there, that is, to comply with the basic minimum standards.

Moreover, minimum standards in housing discouraged the building of low rent, low cost, high density tenements in which most people formerly lived in the central parts of the city, paying something like 15% of their income for shelter. It also discouraged high investment of money or labor in self-help housing which risks being condemned. Thus the cost of slum dwelling increases while its quality further declines.

Government regulations which determine minimum standards for products play right into the hands of the building industry, even when this industry is government controlled. Such regulations effectively lower the total quality of housing as an activity while they render the commodity of housing scarce. Those who produce the commodity get higher salaries or can provide more employment on their staff if they build more and cheaper houses. But almost inevitably even the cheapest house is a commodity for which the poorer half of the population cannot pay.

According to the same study, owner-built houses in the long run are 67% to 89% cheaper than buying in the public sector. In addition, the owner has a maximum incentive, obtains cheap labor, often on the basis of labor exchange. His neighbor works for him during the hours he could not gainfully employ otherwise, and the beneficiary later on works for his neighbor. And above all the builder builds according to his taste and gets satisfaction from dwelling in the shell he has built. He can use the house for several purposes, as a home and a shop, while the public standard commodity does not permit the use of an adjoining cubicle as a pigsty, candy-shop, or shoemaker's workplace.[13]

The only way to improve the process by which most people (in Latin America anyway) shelter themselves, since they cannot get access to professionally-built housing, is to abandon the attempt to provide 'projects' and use the available resources to guarantee people access to plots, tools, materials, and credit. If public resources are to be used for this purpose, it does not make any sense to discuss the lower limits unless upper limits are set on a society-wide basis.

Nobody can provide housing for people, but least of all can anybody provide work, as long as work itself is translated totally as the result of production in a productive institution, and therefore becomes the scarcest of all commodities in a technologically powerful society.

My proposal of a radical new politics setting an upper limit to consumption is not simply neo-Luddite. I do not propose the diminution in numbers of quality of the tools of life. What I do propose is a radical re-evaluation of the part they play in society and the individual's social life.

A society which sets lower limits to the goods and services provided to its members (whether in term of quality or quantity) does not thereby contribute to the conviviality of their lives. On the other hand, a politics of upper limits would supply the individual with maximum power to determine what tools were adapted to his life, to produce and use them for himself and others. A radical new politics would be a politics of conviviality.

Bibliographical notes

Bibliographical notes

1 See for example **H. Fisher**, "The Anatomy of Inflation 1953-1975" in: *The Scientific American*, Nov. 1971.

2 For a conceptual analysis of "Institutional Inversion" see: **H.v.Foerster, I. Illich, H. Maturana, G. Pask.** *Interpersonal Relational Networks*. CIDOC Cuaderno 1014. Cuernarvaca, 1971.

3 For the orientation of readers to in-depth discussion on the crisis of schools in the U.S.A. I recommend:
Michael Mariens, *Alternative Future for Learners*. Educational Policy Research Center. 1206 Harrison Street, Syracuse University, Syracuse, New York. This is an extensive descriptive and critical bibliography of books, articles, and scientific reports which were published during the last five years.
Jordan Bishop. *Schools under Fire:* the Success and the Failure of an Ideology. CIDOC Cuaderno 1015. Apdo. 479. Cuernavaca, Morelos, Mexico. Review of 15 recent books, each characteristic of a different critical approach to the ideology supported by schooling in the U.S.A.
Theodore Rozak *The Making of a Counter Culture:* Reflections on the Technocratic Society and Its Youthful Opposition. Doubleday. New York, 1969. The appendix, pp. 291-303, contains a valuable orientation to the more significant underground currents of educational criticism in the mid-sixties.

4 On "growthmania" see **Prof. Herman E. Daly.** "Towards a Stationary State Economy" in: John Harte and Robert Socolow, ed. *The Patient Earth*. Holt, Rinehart, and Winston, 1971. Also by the same author "On Economics as a Life Science" *Journal of Political Economy*, July, 1968.

5 An excellent introduction to the "Coming Medical War" in the U.S.A. can be found in an article by **Michael Michaelson** in the *New York Review of Books*, July 1st, 1971. He examines nine recent books. The article points towards the demand for profound and urgent reforms which must go far beyond an adaptation to U.S. circumstances or English or Russian prototypes of socialized medicine. But the literature examined still falls short of the demand for the de-professionalization of most functions now performed within the medical-hospital-insurance complex. Literature relevant to this latter question is being reviewed by Prof. John McKnight, Urban Studies, Northwestern University, Evanston, Illinois, and will be published by CIDOC in mid 1972.

On the need for a new conceptual framework for U.S. medicine see also **Harry Schwarz**, "Health Care in America — A Heretical Diagnosis" *Saturday Review*, August 14th, 1971. He states that "if the (now formulated) revolutionary proposals for transforming medicine are adopted, medical care in this country will cost more while providing less satisfaction and poorer treatment for millions."

6 The idea of compulsory school attendance has been generally accepted. I have tried to question its value. Most people in our society would question the value of compulsory medical treatment. I want to point out that in our society medical treatment has become compulsory. Doctors determine increasingly *when* a man must submit to their treatment and *what* treatment he will get.

Legally compulsory consumption of medical services takes various forms: compulsory reclusion in mental hospitals; compulsory medication and supervision by social workers as an alternative to reclusion; compulsory vaccination; hospitalization for childbirth, which in many areas has become inevitable.

Less known, but perhaps more significant as a trend, is the compulsory treatment meted out to children. In July, 1970, President Nixon forwarded a request to the Secretary of Education which recommended that all children henceforth be tested and those found suffering from anti-social or pre-delinquent traits be submitted to remedial treatment, which could be given, if necessary, in special institutions. In the school district of St. Louis, Mo. last year one third of all children with learning difficulties were administered amphetamines provided by school authorities. After protest in the papers, this practice now continues only with the permission of the parents.

Much more widespread than direct compuslion is indirect force applied through subtle monopolistic practices by the medical professions. The imperceptible removal of generics from pharmacy shelves and their substitution by specifics which can be purchased only with prescriptions is a case in point. Another example would be the growth of damage-suits against non-professionals who attempt to provide first-aid in accidents.

The most sinister area of compulsory treatment is probably that provided to the terminally sick.
Frank Turnbull, MD. "Pain and Suffering in Cancer" in: *The Canadian Nurse*. August, 1971. He raises the issue of cancer surgery through which relatively painless death from primary cancer is (sometimes) postponed in exchange for an excruciating death from secondary disease, which is a result of surgical or radiological treatment.

For information on the professional psychological manipulation which U.S. patients undergo to fit them for further consumption of medical services:
E.M.D. Kuebler Ross. *On Death and Dying.* Macmillan, 1969.
Richard A. Kalish. *Death and Dying,* a briefly annotated bibliography. pp. 327-380 in: *The Dying Patient,* ed. by Orville Brim. Russell Sage Foundation. New York, 1970.
Robert Fulton. *Death and Identity.* John Wiley. New York, 1966.

THE ARCHIVES OF THE FOUNDATION OF THANATOLOGY &
JOURNAL OF THANATOLOGY both: 630 W. 168th St. New York
City, New York.

7   I am, of course, arguing here for research on the deprofessionalization
    of clinical diagnosis. But such research can serve a double purpose. It
    can aim at the development of methods to "screen out" healthy people
    from a health-maintenance program (e.g. KAISER PLAN in California).
    It can also aim at the development of diagnostic procedures which lead
    to subsequent non-professionally administered therapy for people who
    will never be able to enter into a client relationship with doctors or
    hospitals.
        Interesting and advanced research is now conducted to achieve the
    first purpose. For technical information consult Dr. William R. Duff
    and Dr. Harry S. Lipscomb at Baylor College of Medicine, Houston,
    Texas. They have devised a 25 minute test-procedure in a laboratory
    furnished with $8,000 of equipment which can be operated by a non-
    professional after short training.
        Much more significant for many more people would be analogous
    research for application in areas where for a generation no medical
    professional will be available for the majority of people.

8   The laws of diminishing returns and increasing destruction of the
    environment apply not only to the industrial production of goods and,
    as we have seen, of services, but also to agriculture. Exhaustion of the
    gene-pool; environmental pollution through fertilizers, pesticides,
    fungicides, insecticides; depletion of the soil and water resources are
    known by-products of the introduction of "miracle" grains. But more
    insidious and destructive is a new form of social stratification: the new
    plants provide disproportionately greater returns for the slightly more
    advantaged farmer. For a summary treatment of the reasons for which
    the "green revolution" threatens the status of the poor farmer, and
    does so everywhere outside of China, see M. Perlemen. "Second
    Thoughts on the Green Revolution" in: *New Republic.* July 17th,
    1971. Norman Borlaug in his Laureate Address upon accepting the
    Nobel Prize recognizes implicitly the arguments advanced by Perlemen.

9   R. Buckminster Fuller, born 1895. Designer of the Geodesic Dome at
    Expo 1967 at the Montreal World Fair; designer of the "Floating City"
    made of ultra-light tetrahedrons which could ultimately house one
    million people in the Bay of Tokyo. Proposes the use of strategic games
    to bring about a world in which technology becomes the servant of
    man, by doing more with less on "Spaceship Earth". He believes that
    reformers err in depending on politics to bring about a better world: "I
    have undertaken the reform of the environment, and never tried to
    reform man '.
        In opposition to Fuller (whom I consider a generally attractive
    though naive representative of a group of unrealistic technological
    futurists) I believe that technology can become man's servant only if
    first a political majority decision determines the technological

parameters within which this can alone be done.

10 According to Staffan Linder an abundance of commodities produces a scarcity of time, partly because it takes time to consume goods and partly because the more productive we are, the more costly is an abstention from production. Hence the richer we get, the less likely we are to give up time to idleness or to apparently unproductive pursuits. **Staffan B. Linder.** *The Harried Leisure Class.* Columbia University Press, 1969.

Kenneth Boulding believes that perhaps the most evident reason for this scarcity of time in developed societies proceeds from the difficulty of economizing time under conditions of long-run commitments to it. He says: "There is a strong tendency for us to overcommit the future, so that when the future becomes present, we seem to be conscious all the time of having an acute scarcity, simply because we have committed ourselves to about thirty hours a day instead of twenty-four. It is this overcommitment which I think creates a sense of pressure and harriedness, rather than the mere fact that time has competitive uses and a high marginal utility in an affluent society."

Life in a society which takes speedy transportation for granted renders time scarce in both of these ways. Activities related to the use of speedy vehicles by *many* people in a society occupy an increasing percentage of the time budget of *most* members of that society, as the speed of the vehicles increases beyond a certain point. Beyond this point the competition of transportation activities with stationary activities becomes fierce, particularly competition over the allocation of limited real-estate, available energy and over life-time. This competition seems to grow exponentially with the rise of speed. Particularly the time reserved for commuting displaces both work and leisure time. Hence, the speedier vehicles are, the more it becomes important that they be constantly filled. (LINDER)

As speed increases, the adaptation of life-patterns to the patterns of vehicles becomes more tyrannical. Here Boulding's argument applies: ". . . we have to make constant corrections and amendments to our allocation of shorter periods. We make appointments and commitments months or even years ahead . . . It is the sense of constant failure which produces a sense of being harried." **(K. Boulding** in: *The New Republic.* February 12th, 1970). I assume that man has only a limited ability to submit to programming. The increase of speed beyond a certain point makes it necessary that the transportation system compete with other systems for human tolerance of social controls.

Increased speed consumes both a larger section of the time-budget *and* adds to the sense of harrassment.

11 Simplification and de-professionalization of technology (for which I argue) must not be confused with a romantic call to return to subsistence agriculture in a pastoral setting, but rather as a condition to make urban life again tolerable. The force of this statement cannot be seized unless we first question two widespread assumptions:

1   that technological advance usually coincides with an improved level of civic and material life within cities

2   that some kind of peasant-culture historically serves as a foundation of city culture.

I am in debt to **Jane Jacobs** for making me question both of these assumptions. *Death and Life of Great American Cities*. Random, 1961. She has shown that 'urban renewal" is usually a euphemism for the the bureaucratically planned destruction of local communities which provide the mainspring of political and economic life for the city.

In her masterly new book *Economy of Cities*. Random, 1969., she argues that in the creation of culture, including agriculture, the city has the pioneer role. Her thesis turns most assumptions on which current urban sociology and economy is based upside down.

Another important argument is made by **Milton Kotler.** *Neighborhood Governments: the local foundation of political life* , 1969. On the hand of historical research he shows that the institutionalization of service-needs (care of the sick, the mad, the jobless, the alcoholic), after a certain size has been reached in the organization, always reduces the amount of service available, and leads to "downtown imperialism" over depoliticized suburbs.

12 Another objection often raised to building self-limiting criteria into institutions is based on a spurious ethological assumption: the hypothesis of an innate instict of mutual aggression in the human species. The consequences which one can draw, starting from this ideology, were brilliantly drawn by **Leonard C. Levin.** *Report from Iron Mountain*: on the Possibility and Desirability of Peace. Dial Press, 1967.

The "Report" pretends to be a suppressed U.S. Government Document arguing that the world would face an unparalleled catastrophe if permanent peace should "break out". The document deals with the "non-military purposes of warmaking". It argues that social stability has always been based on a war-system. According to the report, it is a general assumption that war, as an institution, is subordinate to the social system which it serves. And the Report arrives at the conclusion that this assumption is wrong: war itself is the basic social system.

The Report is a disturbing and logical caricature. The ideology which the report portrays has received wide circulation through such people as zoologist **Konrad Lorenz** *(On Aggression)* and writers like **Robert Ardrey** *(African Genesis, The Territorial Imperative)*.

Unfortunately this same argument comes up frequently in discussion to 'prove' that open-ended escalating competition in peaceful enterprise is a crucial condition to divert human aggressivity from mutual destruction.

Anthony Storr. *Human Aggression.* Atheneum, 1968, shows that nearly all the "lower" orders of animals enact the ritual of conflict, but that man stands almost alone among the species in this propensity to destroy others of his kind systematically. **Dr. Erich Fromm** is now putting the last corrections to a manuscript in which he shows that specifically human aggressiveness develops only with the private appropriation of tools and land during the neolithic period.

For our argument we can put into parenthesis the question about the origins of human aggression, and simply focus on the fact that humans, as we now know them, do find important outlets for their aggression through institutional channels. Storr's contribution to my central thesis lies in the fact that he shows how the need for "upper limits" and the need for effective channelling of aggression are related.

He points out that one crucial psychological and social cost of complex and highly centralized organizational arrangements is the growing inability of such institutions to serve as channels for meaningful personal aggression.

Institutions cannot serve for such conflict resolution if they are large and complex beyond a certain point. This point, very frequently, lies much below the point at which the institutions can be competitive in economic terms with the output of larger producers. The acceptance of limits on some dimensions of institutional products is therefore one of the radical devices by which productive institutions can again serve their most fundamental psychological and social functions.

Storr points out that without recognition and personal experience of the legitimacy of conflict among humans, there is no formal democratic setting in which to establish selfhood, or in which to discover what is rational in an opponent's view. I argue that such recognition and experience becomes impossible when, for productivity's sake, institutions are forced to grow beyond a certain point.

13 It is important to distinguish clearly between a technology designed for the progressive de-professionalization of major service-areas, and one designed for use by new para-professions.

For documentation of the trend towards proliferation of monopolies which control knowledge see **Amitai Etzioni.** *The Semi-professions and Their Organization.* Free Press, 1969.

For the medical sector specifically: **Eliot Freidson,** *Professional Dominance:* the Social Structure of Medical Care. Atherton Press, 1970.

For the professionalization under the protection of the "counselling ideology" in psychiatric, educational, and social-work areas see **Paul Hamos.** *The Personal Service Society.* Schocken, 1970.

The Writers and Readers Publishing Cooperative

was formed in the autumn of 1974.

We are a cooperative collectively owned and operated by its worker-members, several of whom are writers.

We are members of the Industrial Common Ownership Movement.

Our policy is to encourage writers to assume greater control over the production of their own books; and teachers, booksellers and readers generally to engage in a more active relationship with publisher and writer.

We attempt to keep our overheads as low as possible so as to keep our book prices down, and thereby benefiting readers.

We welcome response which will tell us what readers wish to read.

If you would like to be put on our mailing list and receive regular information about our books, please write to:

Writers and Readers Publishing Cooperative
144a Camden High Street, London NW1
175 Fifth Avenue, New York. NY 10010